SO SPOKE PENELOPE

ALSO BY TINO VILLANUEVA

Hay Otra Voz Poems (*1968-1971*) (Madrid-New York: Editorial Mensaje, 1972; third printing 1979)

Shaking Off the Dark (Houston: Arte Público Press, 1984; revised edition, Tempe: Bilingual Press, 1998)

Crónica de mis años peores (La Jolla: Lalo Press, 1987; third printing, Madrid: Editorial Verbum, 2001)

Chronicle of My Worst Years (Evanston: Northwestern University Press, 1994), bilingual edition of *Crónica de mis años peores*, translated with an Afterword by James Hoggard

Scene from the Movie GIANT (Willimantic: Curbstone Press, 1993; fourth printing 2006; currently under the imprint of Northwestern University Press)

Escena de la película GIGANTE (Madrid: Editorial Catriel, 2005), translated by Rafael Cabañas Alamán

Primera causa / First Cause (Merrick, NY: Cross-Cultural Communications, 1999; second printing, 2004), translated by Lisa Horowitz

SO SPOKE PENELOPE

Tino Villanueva

GROLIER POETRY PRESS
Cambridge, Massachusetts

ACKNOWLEDGMENTS

Grateful acknowledgment to the editors of the following journals in which these poems, some in slightly different form, first appeared:

Poiesis: A Journal of the Arts and Communication, Vol. 6 (2004): "So Spoke Penelope," "Prayer to Athena," "Dream," "In Color and in Cloth" and "A Width of Cloth"

Bagels with the Bards: Bagelbard Anthology, No. 2 (2007): "Shining Through"

Quale America? Soglie e culture di un continente, Vol. 2 (Daniela Ciani Forza, editor; 2007): "Patterns That I Weave," "This Day" and "Today I Did Almost Nothing"

Wilderness House Literary Review, Vol. 2, No. 3 (Fall 2007), http://www.whlreview.com: "This Thirsting Earth"

The Loyalhanna Review (2007): "The Waiting" and "When It Is Time"

Ibbetson Press: Selected Works (2008), http://www.ibbetsonpress.com/ImaginingOdysseus.html: "Imagining Odysseus"

Shabdaguchha (April–June 2008): "How I Wait" and "Possessed by Doubt"

The Seventh Quarry, Issue Eight (Summer 2008): "Just as the Sea" and "Come to Me"; idem., Issue Nine (Winter 2008): "In the Courtyard"

Camino Real: Estudios de las Hispanidades Norteamericanas, Vol. I, Núm. 1 (2009): "Shining Like the Sea," "Sometimes in Quietude," "The Suitors," "Wakeful Dreaming" and "Love Bound"

Ibbetson Street, No. 28 (2010): "Against All Odds"

Printed for the Grolier Poetry Press, Cambridge, Massachusetts by Thomson-Shore Inc., Dexter, Michigan

CONTENTS

INTRODUCTION

I begin by noting that, from where I stand, I am quite fascinated by the fact that Tino Villanueva has dared to take on the Penelope story in the first place. And that he has done so with such loving attention and emotional range, and with such an unscripted natural ease, is all the more extraordinary. Over the centuries, the Penelope story has attracted many, but most of those attracted either have resided closer to the center of the story's telling, or else have had other personal or professional reasons for being so moved. The question, then, for many of us who know Villanueva's work, or know him personally, comes to this: why this attention to the Penelope story? Is this just another poetic project of the author, or does the poet have something else up his sleeve?

Lest the reader be tempted to think that Villanueva simply woke up one morning and decided to do the Greek Penelope thing, let the reader think again. For what we have in *So Spoke Penelope* is a work many years in the making, a work indicative of a hard-won recognition on the poet's part, as Werner Sollors has put it, "that the whole range of human experience is contained in Penelope at Ithaca." Here, I suspect that this work will become an important part of a growing body of work defining a new aesthetics—an aesthetics that is right and appropriate for our distended modern world, and is based on a shared magnanimity of spirit, on a stubborn awareness that each of our cultures drawn in onto itself can only accomplish so much, but that when nations learn to sing each other's songs, then we are on our way to something magnificent, something perhaps ultimately sublime.

With wisdom and an adept style, Villanueva has managed in this work to negotiate his way through the many polarities that bedevil us—male vs. female, West vs. non-West, old times vs. new times. The poet has been a bridge builder. Certainly, these categories listed above are categories of understanding, none of which is adequate to apprehend the complexities of the world we live in, and each of which, taken alone, betrays the spirit of what is collectively possible. Of course, one does not write poetry by committee. But poets, we assume, function like some sort of priest-figures. And if a priest, called upon to take care of the spiritual needs of a large community, were instead to insist on taking care of the spiritual needs of members of his or her immediate family, then this priest-person had better give up the profession, go into another one, say, the digging of ditches or the picking of plums. To the extent that poets are deeply entangled in this ancient organism called language, an organism that predates all their individual lives, to that extent do they have to remain loyal to the nobility of their calling, whether they are so inclined or not. Part of their job is to speak and show us the way. In my mind, *So Spoke Penelope* has answered a priestly call; it is a book so obviously blessed with a generous spirit. Its reach and underlying surprises should make us proud, should give one hope that our stubborn divisions will one day cease.

As editor of the Grolier Poetry Series, I have sometimes jokingly said to friends and acquaintances alike that my job now is to begin the process of abolishing all tribalism in poetry. How do you do that, Mr. Editor, my friends have asked? And what exactly do you mean by this tribalism in poetry that needs to be abolished? Tell us what you mean and we will join you in the fight. In answer I have said to them that the details are still being filled in. In any case, *So Spoke Penelope*, in my mind, is a step in this very direction.

For Villanueva the poet, before there was a Penelope of Ithaca, there was another Penelope of the hard Texas sun. I have in mind Villanueva's earlier tribute to the extraordinary patience and enduring love of his own grandmother, Clara Solana Ríos, born in Eagle Pass, Texas, 1885 and died in San Marcos, Texas, in 1965. The grit and resolve of this simple woman, born to hardship on the Mexican border but determined that hardship should not overwhelm her offspring, as she went about patiently trying to feed and protect her own, was very much in evidence. This patient determination has been eloquently captured by Villanueva in his poem "Now, Suns Later" which appeared in the collection *Shaking Off the Dark*, published in 1984. I believe that Clara Solana Ríos, in her own way, has been part of the poet's journey towards this other Penelope made famous since the early times of Greek history. No one who has not found strength at home will find strength when he decides to go abroad at some later time. The journey is one of a kind, and what I am proposing is that the reason *So Spoke Penelope* is as strong as it is can be traced to the fact that Villanueva has circled this territory before, circled it from within the bounds of family love.

Of Clara Solana Ríos, Villanueva has written that her "yielding belly put nine screaming mouths / at a simple table. / She left no one unweaned, unwanted, / was up before the sun struck dawn / kneading *tortillas* / to keep a race going." Clara, we learn, was also a weaver of sorts, who wove from some of the cotton she had picked "by the baleful," and whose "threads like rainbows gave shape to warmth. / From ready remnants, she patterned light glowing quilts; / from remnants of remnants she braided a rug. / And pillows, high and ruffled, came from feathers / of Sunday chickens." Age, of course, eventually began to catch up with Clara, and her arms became weary, "[h]er slim life bending like a corn stalk, / fragile, in the middle of a spring wind...". And with these memories still an important part of the adult Villanueva's life, he writes:

> Still her memory warms the day for me.
> And I endure,
> for patience must have been her only strength,
> her only movement, truly private.
> Lonely.

Which of course brings me back to that earlier point about abolishing tribalism in poetry. The point, again, is that the poet, having opened his heart in homage to a dear grandmother, whose long-suffering patience under the hard Texas sun he so clearly admired, how could he now close off his heart, his sympathetic interest, to that other Penelope from literary history, the Penelope of Ithaca? One would have to be an incorrigible tribalist to even begin to attempt such a split of affections. Surely, any poet worth his credentials (once he is aware of these issues) is going to try very hard to avoid any such debilitating split in the affective sources that motivate all poetry.

For, in this particular business of poetry, it appears to me that the more we are willing to reach out beyond our isolated domains, the more, also, we are able to secure the foundations on which we stand, locally. After all, language is something akin to a magisterium, expansive in its powers; it is not a mechanism for fencing off discrete little enclaves, each one set apart from the other, and each an abode where only little things are allowed to happen. Surely, the human spirit is larger than that, and its language should not be confined as if it belonged with clueless little chickens running around in isolated village settings, unaware of the highway beyond the gates.

Finally, let me turn my attention to one other item. It is to Villanueva's other outreach poem, also indicative of an admirable generosity of spirit, which appeared in the *Partisan Review* (No. 4, 1997) and deals with the Holocaust. The poem is titled "At the Holocaust Museum: Washington D.C.". In it the poet, turning his attention to humanity's various "declensions of rage" and the unavoidable "conclusion mortality demands," writes:

> Then there was Ejszyszki (A-shish-key), 1941:
> a village of 4,000 that could not find the
> doors to exodus—slaughtered in two days.
> I touch the photographs of how it was
> before it ended in a great field of darkness...
> and my body shrieks.
> Five decades, and in another country,
> I am too late as in a blazing nightmare
> where I reach out,
> but cannot save you, cannot save you.
> *Sarah, Rachel, Benjamin*, in this light you have risen
> where the past is construed as present.
> For all that is in me: let the dead go on living,
> let these words become human.
>
> I am your memory now.

What I have tried to do in this Introduction is to show the affinities, the natural trajectory, to Villanueva's undertaking in this matter of Penelope of Ithaca. At this point, let me rest my case and let the reader begin the reading of the poems in *So Spoke Penelope*.

Ifeanyi Menkiti
December 2012

I wish to thank R. Hadas, L. Horowitz, and A. E. Stallings for their useful comments and suggestions on the early drafts of some of these poems.

My deepest gratitude to R. C. Clawson, J. Martino, E. Vandiver, and M. C. Wheeler who read and critically remarked on the complete version of the manuscript.

Grateful appreciation likewise to the Ledig-Rowohlt Foundation and their Maison d'écrivains for granting this writer a residency at a critical juncture in the life of this book.

SO SPOKE PENELOPE

SO SPOKE PENELOPE

This is the palace where I've learned to survive;
where two years ago I embraced Odysseus,
stout son of Laertes, one last time—
one long embrace was all it took
to shape one heartbeat between us before he left for Troy.

This is the palace I walk around in
from hall to hall, a world of stone and wood that is mine.
This is the room where I work in wool,
and talk it out with myself;
where still awake I toss and turn,
pace around in the middle of the night,
convincing myself once more
that the earthly idea of love is still the life-blood of my body.

This is the palace where I wear the crown of faithfulness;
where the sound of the sea is the sound I think with.
Therefore, if I stand by a window expecting each time to see
the outline of a ship coming toward me,
what is it but my love,
and the passion time gives it to grow for Odysseus,
like-minded husband of the cunning mind, for whom I wait.

So spoke Penelope when she awoke this morning;
when the golden cloth of dawn rose
out of the sea.

THE WAITING

Has ever a woman waited like me…
waited and waited and,
if she hadn't,
would've had too much to lose—
would've been denied so terribly a husband,
not to mention orchards, many,
droves of sheep and swine, plow-fields all around,
and twining vines for wine?

How many women, I wonder, have waited like me,
like me by the sea, with a racing caring heart,
women who waited, stood waiting,
lay waiting like me?

From where you are every night above me,
tell me with your truthful mouth, Sky-God Zeus,
tell it clearly to me, Athena and Apollo, luminous
gods and goddesses who inhabit the high halls of Olympus,

how many women before me
have waited like me?

HOW I WAIT

Today I sit by a window, my spirit
swimming out into the deep-azure-blue of the sea.
I'm a woman waiting, in love with a man,
and in love with the love we had.
I took an oath with myself to wait,
and keep passionately waiting
even after the great shining of the sun has worn away.

I pick up my sorrow and carry it to bed,
and wait some more
before sweet sleep weighs down my eyes.
Next day I rise,
and hear myself speaking words of all-abounding hope
...and go on waiting. These things I say aloud
to have clear thought,
to keep the day alive.

I'm a woman waiting,
waiting with the restlessness of sea-waves
repeating themselves in her head
like messages from afar.

IMAGINING ODYSSEUS

Day after day, my days are alike
as the grinding and sifting of barley and wheat;
and times without number I've sighted Odysseus,
man of the manly build,
walking out of gray fog over the sea
from a journey too long to tell about
in a single night.
I am but dreaming when I see him walking with a purpose
this way toward the palace:

> don't break stride through unfinished distance, say I,
> in one quick breath,
> wishing my words had the wing-beat of geese
> at break of day.
> I'm upstairs...here, take lovingly in your arms me.

After so long and this much said,
reason strikes me, as light shines on water, that his journey
won't end until he makes his way into our room,
lies in this tree-trunk bed
set down with the love we both expect.

PATTERNS THAT I WEAVE

Five years.
Five years my mind has wandered,
strayed off into a forest of confusion and more than once
lost its way back over rocky hills.

If only Odysseus,
man of the valorous will, could know my heart now beats
in two directions,
that back-and-forth I love him...I love him not:
I love him, and easily undo patterns that I weave;
I hate him, and do nothing else but weave
over-and-under-across-and-through-and-deep into the night.
I rest the shuttle to one side, and rub my hands,
and grow each day impatient—
I wasn't born to bear a harried heart.

Finally, at the moment of sleep when
flickering torch-lights are snuffed out,
one thought, irresistible, comes to me:

gods and goddesses—
it can't be said that they exist.
May one day their names be forgotten.

SHINING LIKE THE SEA

Because love seeks out love,
deserves to be loved in several ways,
Odysseus, to whom I gave my heart freely,
knows he must return,
knows there's much between us
that remains.

I cannot hide these thoughts, not now
as the solitary, vast, red-round sun
sinks. Here I go once more, demanding
what I can of love that way,
by which I mean
               love of the grandest kind—

heart-felt love,
up-and-down-my-body love.

AGAINST ALL ODDS

Did Odysseus, man of thoughts
accurate as arrows, win the battle?
Were he and his warring men victorious?
    If so, let him conquer distance now—
    to Ithaca he must come back.

Six years it's been,
and who now cares who started the war?
Cannot the gods bring on all-out peace?
    Enough with this madness.
    I, Penelope, his wife, want him back.

Was he captured, taken prisoner? Is he
trapped in a deep-shaded forest...
concealed in a cave not knowing east from west?
    Against all odds, against whatever gods,
    he'd better make it back.

On his homeward sail,
was he blown off course by blasting gales,
his ship lost in some outer world?
    May he use whatever stars are in him
    to turn around and get back.

Is he shipwrecked, bruised
by the perils of the sea against some rocky shore...
or else swept out into the streams of Ocean?
    I beseech you, gods Olympian: release him
    from all trouble, and help him find his way back.

After all the fruitless years,
it weighs on my wit:
has he found...settled down with another woman?

I'll take him back—
Telemachus and I need him back.

In the end, did he breathe his last in battle...
is he dead and buried, olive trees growing
among his bones?
    I pray to the deathless gods that round out the heavens
to bring his body back.

SHINING THROUGH

The wind blows,
and I can hear the leaves of orchards breathing.
On days like today I head outdoors
(with me follow three maids),
and welcome the plentiful draft of cool air full of sea.
Stone-tough is my hope this day, tough as Ithaca's bedrock
where I step.
O calm hope that carries me through.

Here I celebrate the red orb of morning
sliding out of the water, filling day with light.
Would that I could catch sight of a ship with taut sails,
well-made oars like wings flying toward me
manned by Odysseus out of the blue,
the man who in a cloud of dust won me in a footrace...
the man I learned to love and follow.

O brimming joy!—here I stand
full of plans for the day my husband
once more claims Ithaca home.
Even on days driven by rain,
dull-gray in the morning, storm-fed gray in the afternoon,
my lightning thoughts tell of signs I'm alive.
As long as the sun rises,
as long as olive trees grow, and geese occupy the sky
I shall ever look toward the sea for Odysseus,
man whose spirit shines through.

Now and then I'm convinced—
hope is a goddess looking over me.

PRAYER TO ATHENA

Blesséd goddess Athena, I come to you as suppliant.
Hear out each bit of my complaint:
first two, then five,
now nine years I have waited with all my might for Odysseus
to return from war, proper husband I am constant to
as the sun each day takes the sky
—nine years with no end in sight.
I know nothing of his whereabouts, nor if, in fact,
he ever reached Troy.
From this end of the earth on Ithaca, I turn to you for help
although nine years mean nothing to you,
and little to eternity.

How long must I keep company with my irritable self,
trapped in whichever palace room I roam,
made worse when my body moves in rhythm
as if in tribute to the moon?
At times I cannot even work the loom—
a cloth, half-finished, sits waiting for its other half
in a corner of the room; nor can I rid myself
of things familiar that take me by surprise:
wind-storms bring on nightmares of victims of a shipwreck;
the quietest of rain can bring on tears.

Pallas Athena, guardian of the glinting-eyes,
drop down from the clouds, and instruct me.
Reverse my tears, send me consoling dreams.
Otherwise, what am I to do—ten times repeat a prayer
at the altar-stone of Zeus? Or at the water's edge sacrifice a ram
to your uncle ranked with the immortals, Poseidon,
deep-down ruler of the sea?

Athena, send me a god or goddess who can guide my destiny
into the open arms of joy of dear Odysseus,
more than just a man—my husband, and father to my boy.

THIS DAY

This dull day
this dreary day
this bleak day

this irritable day
this worrisome day
this fretful day
this exasperating day
this wretched day
this tormenting day

this joyless, dismal day
this somber day
this weary day
this doleful day

this empty day
this inconsolable day
this depressing day
this pointless, ordinary day

this day

DREAM

I reach up
  and feel I am climbing,
climbing threads.
  I climb short ones
—and stop.
  Some feel like ropes,
which I climb and climb.
  I cross over to grab another,
and climb some more.
  I climb and keep climbing
and come to what looks
  like a mountainside
ready to be climbed.
  I step off and begin to climb it.
I climb past four eagles nesting that
  fly away in different directions.
I climb and climb
  rugged steeps of rock and brush
until I hit cloud-cover looming,
  turning into the shape of darkness:
darkness crowding together,
  then separating; crowding together,
separating.
  I climb and arrive at a place
where people find light:
  darkness above me;
light straight below.
  There I go falling,
falling down a tangle of threads.
  I grab one and hang on to it,
and then another,
  and begin to descend
like descending down ropes

    toward a bright field of waking.
I've come back,
    back through the lightness of light
that astounds me.
    I climbed and climbed, and was there—
I was there, I tell you,
    and saw what I saw as clear as the loom
here before me, here in sunlight.

SOMETIMES, IN QUIETUDE

I lie awake and turn it over in my head
that waiting for a man twelve years is useless.
A man away that long
should have the heart to send word home.
Othertimes I try to have no thoughts at all, no thoughts
on what the Fates are spinning out for young Telemachus,
and me;
on whether I can find it in myself to honor custom—
to take another man in marriage, a father for my son,
withdraw completely from this place,
and not look back.

Nights, I try to find deep sleep, which easily
doesn't come.
Worst the nights of cold and frost when my longing
drags my spirit down to the stony floor, the air
moving through the branches
jangling my nerves.
In bed beside me—great gods in the morning,
I'm married to the passing of time! What bliss is this,
counting the years in the dark...useless time
like a living thing I can't escape?

Warm nights are not much better
when tormentor Aphrodite overwhelms me
at the slightest movement I might make,
or when a lulling, loving breeze slips in through the window
and has its way with me, wandering all along my naked skin.
How much are you a wife, my spirit finally asks,
if tomorrow you relent and take another man as mate?
Not much, comes my reply,
not much if you cast too soon bright hope aside.

And so I wait along the sands...and keep on
waiting for the whims of the gods,
the rocking motion of the sea
to issue up a man as much in love with me
as I with him.

IN COLOR AND IN CLOTH

It's done—finished.
Three days ago, as an impatient sun was dropping fast
behind the sea,
and a starlit sky appeared, I finished it—
a piece of cloth in wool that took too long to weave.
Half a year dragged on, but at last I have it:
the likeness of Odysseus,
splendid husband and gentle father to his infant son.
One day I managed from early dawn to dusk,
then until the brightness of the morning shone again
to keep on weaving, to get it right. And there it is
folded up across the bed in color and in cloth.

Now, when the sting of absence is too much,
when the weariness of why-keep-waiting wears me out,
I reach for it to satisfy my love-struck eyes.
The background: I've simply made it dark,
against which stands Odysseus looking rapt into my eyes.
Beside us, our longest table in the palace hall, and
because he's speaking to me,
I gave him speaking lips. He's telling me he doesn't
care for war, that he loves me "to the Pleiades and back."
In turn, I'm offering wine to him from my wooden bowl.
Standing there,
long pose from each of us
is what I remember most: he and I glowing
from two bowls of sweet and mellow wine.

Need I say I pleasure in bringing out this piece of cloth—
such felicity unfolding it,
running my hands over it, and embracing
both ourselves each time.

WHEN IT IS TIME

Down the path toward the shore
past olive trees and barely-living grass between stones,
I among maidservants
glance out over water,
and thrill to realize the presence of the sea with birds
gliding in the sustaining air—
wind enough for sails of a worthy vessel to sail home.

Sights like these hearten me to keep waiting for Odysseus,
husband whose love was like rain
breathing life into the earth.
And there I shall be like a farmer
waiting for fruit to fall when it is time.

How long, I ask myself, can I bear up
to Aphrodite's visitation that drives me to headaches...
makes me faint at the knees.
In the name of love and things that go on living,
O that Odysseus, sunrise of my life,
could heed my call, rise out of the sea;
that I could shut my eyes and bring him to me
in goddess-like thought;
that I could touch and be touched with love saved up
year-upon-year,
letting my body burn into him and together be one.

Still and all, what to do when love washes over me
head to toe,
my body awake as sea-waves that do not sleep?
Does any god care about us mortals in love,
care that love loves to be loved, but by the right lover?

For the moment, may Aphrodite keep her distance,
and not seize me in her grip,
for that's when I unravel and doubt my gift as wife,
the wife of irresistible Odysseus, complete and shining husband,
the man, as much now as then, I love.

THIS THIRSTING EARTH

Clouds and more clouds. All these I see
laid out, barely moving, flat-gray all of them,
quickly darkening,
and soon enough everything is ominous in slow flight.
They ebb and flow,
                              stream along and swirl as well,
gathering up like flocks of sheep around the sun,
barely letting happiness shine through.

Then came today when clouds took up every bit of sky—
one vast extension of gray,
like the surf rolled in,
hanging there on nothing, wanting to
drop rain.

Here on Ithaca, alas, we had no favoring rain today,
no sun.
And I, who am Penelope, living mother of a living son,
neither got Odysseus back,
husband whose love I miss on awakening,
nor chose to take a suitor as my man.

Rain-God Zeus, do send rain when the thirsting earth
feels deprived.
Make it a cloudburst, a downpour with lightning strokes
if you choose,
and a rumble of thunder
                              to make me feel alive.

POSSESSED BY DOUBT

Do not be cross with me, Odysseus,
source of my worry and my woe,
if by and by I loathe you for the anxious nights
you give me, nights that wreck me to the core.
What's more and must be said in this battlefield of love:
time and time again I love you,
then I go the other way
              and love you not.

Day in, day out, each day that travails me
when I feel denied, when
my unsleeping thoughts go round and round my head,
I cry out your name as if it were honey
on my tongue—the sound resounding in this room,
giving hope to this island realm, and me, alone.
Whereupon I smile to swallows
high in the warm air, going past with a will to fly.
Soon after in the spread of stars
              I find reason to love you,
and then another...and another.

Still and all, Odysseus,
grief-giver of a husband, destroyer of hearts,
let me not die aching in one place.
I loathe you for your absence, for the sorrow
that lowers me to bed weeping;
for keeping Telemachus, our son,
and me, your wife, waiting;
for sending no message down the years—
no final word to soothe this range of anger,
this heart beginning now to be possessed by doubt.

IN THE COURTYARD

On a perfectly serene and splendid day,
as it was today when my spirit soared with the sun,
and now sails with the stars,
Odysseus, the great attainment of my life,
will set his sights on home
as swallows will from higher air,
to Ithaca return, to this kingdom,
this palace, to me—of this I'm convinced.
Once in my arms, husband only one, lover only one,
we shall reverse the failure of fifteen years
without each other, for love touches those
who've loved before.

Such endless thoughts I can't refuse tonight—
the Pleiades above,
and three handmaidens at my side.
All sleepiness withdraws as we stroll past Zeus' altar,
breathe in the coolness of the air,
the instant brightened to its brightest.
O glorious Pleiades drawn against the sky,
which I can only see by stepping out into the night,
I accept your light with open arms.

May affectionate, great-hearted Odysseus
reach up with his eyes as I tonight
to the far-away star-shine of the sky.
Let the Pleiades be the place where we both meet
as in a kind of dream—
husband and wife wishing on the same thing.

A WIDTH OF CLOTH

Give me the craft of weaving, more subtle than working with bronze; stone's too brutish, too heavy, too cold. A piece of cloth: first I make it in my mind and keep it there, blending in the figures and designs against the background that I want, adding and subtracting as I please, sitting with my thoughts; which is to say, a width of cloth of any type starts with nothing, if nothing is whatever an empty, wooden, upright loom is set to hold. The thrill of yarn comes later when, finally, I've chosen from a basketful of unshaped, jumbled colors of spun threads, mindful that the riper colors are sometimes best; yet, with the blush of others, a warmer light fulfills the eye as well. Then, and only then, with confidence, do I push the shuttle through, over-and-under-up-and-down-and-back-and-forth. It's not easy turning feelings into cloth. But once I make my way into the work, each time I weave the strands across-and-through, and tie-and-knot-and-cut-and-weave some more, the worthiness of cloth tightens as when any bard takes a story and lifts it into song, word-on-word strung around the strumming of his lyre. Phase by phase I shape it into the world I know—I can see it, and my fingers know it when the yarn slips through them many times and more, fingers working spider-like. When I think I'm through, I'm not, which makes me take a different turn where I unweave, change the pattern of the lines, draw another color in. And I alone working, keep within this room with such driven-woman diligence that, at times, I fail to eat and, for a moment, whatever ails me is no more. I thank the gods I have no bronze to beat or bend; no block of stone to punish. O blessèd be the craft of weaving, more subtle than working with bronze. Stone's too brutish, too heavy, too cold.

JUST AS THE SEA

Cast your eyes in my direction,
gods who reside in the upper deep;
give me the solitude without the loneliness
as the sun sinks fast beyond the sea,
then see how much I am drowning on this island,
my need to hope so hungry
I quiver with unrest.

Once more the pears and pomegranates ripened;
the vines have given up their fruit...
and one more year, the seventeenth, is almost in decline.
The next day Ithaca keeps burning in the sun
with so much water shining round it,
its rocky hills thirsting for cool rain.
If I, Penelope, could dream the dreams of the sea,
and have the water speak to me the secrets it may hold,
then might I find my way to Odysseus,
husband handsomest of all.

Give me a sign, dear gods just over the horizon,
that my husband will step off his lean, black ship one day,
will make Ithaca once more his home
just as the sea each day mounts the shore
and loves it.

TODAY I DID ALMOST NOTHING

Today
I dwelt in my room...did almost nothing.
Kindest woman Eurycleia brought me food,
which I took in bed—cheese and honey, a piece of barley
bread.
A blank tapestry of day went by, colorless,
inspiring nothing, revealing nothing.
I renewed myself in a clean tunic,
and thinking all around I thought about Odysseus,
husband beloved who, when we kissed, made love swell
inside me.
Thought about war
...war that spoils the ties of love and mocks my marriage;
thought about this palace, life without it
should it come down to marrying a suitor;
hoped, too truly, my son will not lose out
on his royal rights from birth—
cattle grazing,
sheep and goats aplenty,
plow-lands everywhere and bounty on them.

Today
I kept to my upstairs room where I didn't work in wool,
gave no orders to house servants to draw water
from the spring.
From the big hall down below:
the lordly suitors,
their low-slung utter drifting up into my room.
A milder light of twilight came, and stayed awhile;
the cicada's chirring stopped.
From my window: the calm eternity of the sea
went out of sight.
I must've muttered something, for then I heard

much-knowing devoted Eurycleia:
"...and twice you sighed, good queen,
while staring out the window. Such long despair
I've never heard before."

Today I awoke,
and looked forward to nothing in the day at all—
the sun came up,
the sun went down.
The day went like that.

GOD OF EXTENDED BLUE WATERS

Poseidon, God of Extended Blue Waters,
hear me out. The ships I see
a great way off
make the heart soar on wings of contentment.
Their shapes arise shimmering on water,
and I pray to the all-imposing gods
that Odysseus, husband of the steadfast mind,
commands one, and leads the way home.
A certain joyfulness enters the room,
and for a moment grief subsides,
all misery lifted from me.
Alas, ships sail on past Ithaca.

Just yesterday, late afternoon,
thick fog on the ground having lifted:
three serving-girls joined me for a walk
along the shore and the sounding of the sea.
We heard the slam of surf
against dumb rock,
the swishing to-and-fro of foam.
The wide way of the sea was before us,
when a glint of hope showed through
from the deepest part of distance.
We didn't have to strain to see it twice
...and once again—mast and sail perhaps;
sun striking oars in-and-out of water.
The maidservants swore they were ships.
So did I.

To have seen what I saw,
then have it turn to haze or mist—O Poseidon,
all hope went under...I blinked a tear,
cursed the open sea in one long breath.

I know now you were behind it,
and false hopes that ache on me
I do not need. Things like that age a woman.
And that rainbow afterwards—
you sent it, I daresay, to spite me. If this be true:
into the bottom-most pit of the sea with you.

Hear me now, Earth Shaker God,
tease me not with the falsehood of your waves;
no more tricks from you—play not with my heart.
Keep away the awful plotting that you weave
into the fabric of my days
                                        already worn, and frayed.

ANOTHER PRAYER TO ATHENA

Shining-eyed Athena, favorite daughter of Zeus,
may these words reach you at the speed of my voice,
and make sense as threads gathered on a loom.
For eighteen years Odysseus,
husband who sails in my mind against a sky set blue,
has been gone.
As for the sea swaying, forever alive—
it answers me nothing,
only ships ghosting-up in mist that do not stop,
ships as close as my voice can carry in the wind.
And that mocking throng of suitors,
low and gross,
keeps wearing down my patience.
I turn away from them, and ask myself:
what duties should now my life
obey, those of a widow
or those of a wife?

More than once, Athena, I have felt
the weariness of land-life, the pull of the sea.
If only I were not mortal, not a woman,
I would command ships
to far-lying islands, and with me Telemachus,
a crew of men and women: Eurycleia,
whose mind knows many things; fifty maidservants;
Eumaeus too, and faithful herdsman Philoetius,
and binder of words Phemius,
court herald Medon, and old man Dolius—
to look for Odysseus, man of lovingkindness,
and to whom I owe this woe.

Athena, third-born daughter of Zeus,
speak to my mind and tell me life will soon be sweetness;
that before long, I pray,
my river of sorrow will run into his sea of love,
breaking over me wave after wave...

THE SUITORS

Those blasted blustery brutes:
the crudest of the crude crowding my thoughts.
Rain or shine,
it's them again—rowdy louts befouling the air
with the rough language of their praise.
From up here
they're sound in my ears, pure chatter,
low-cunning boastful men who wear no patience
...loud, saying nothing that matters.

Me, I've grown stubborn all these years. As have they.
The more I refuse them the more they desire me on and on
as they would sweet figs glowing
in someone else's orchard,
fruit they'll never eat,
all the while emptying the larders, butchering my cattle,
swilling my wine.
The mess they daily make
my poor maidservants unmake with the same sore hands
that scrub the floor and grind the grain.

What remarkable occurrence, indeed,
if I could lead them to a crossing point,
a contest of some sort—a test of strength of much devising,
where each would fall or fail into defeat.
After all, not one suitor I'd want to hug to my breast:
not brash Amphinomus, not Eurymachus nor Antinous.
One delightful day, if I can hold my ground,
I shall greatly welcome
                    their departure.

I may, on occasion, groom myself to strike a better presence—
to look attractive, you might say,
and so they gaze their fill whenever I'm downstairs.
How flattered they must feel
thinking I'm doing it for them.
But little do they realize
when they see me smiling through my veil,
that I'm smiling with my mouth,
not with my eyes.

At last—at last it's night,
and each suitor has repaired to his home, out of sight.

I breathe the fresh, clean air.

COME TO ME

Come to me
as a far-away star would reach me, Odysseus,
husband whose love alone allays me.
Come to me as a jolt of hope through darkness.

Come to me as moonlight, or a bright sun,
or simply as light from palace torches at night
cast upon the work of hands on wool, upon my loom.

Come to me as glistening waves advancing evermore
toward the shore.

Come to me in whichever radiance of light you desire.

PHEMIUS, THE BARD

Phemius, the bard,
was singing to a crowd of suitors today.
I could hear him from my upstairs room,
singing of ancient peoples warring,
going on about who won, who lost, who fell
slaughtered to the ground,
dragging and drowning his voice for effect,
bringing the right hurt
to the notes.
No sooner had he finished with the past
than he shifted to the present, taking distance away
to make us feel the battlefield at Troy—
no doubt he knew his song well before singing.
What Phemius doesn't realize:
I can do without the outburst of his words;
people have not always relished war,
and the rage of armies clashing gives me pain.
Why sing that dead and bloodied flesh is what remains
for carrion birds and fierce dogs snarling?

So too his lyre, tuned tight,
was grating on my nerves.
He struck no errant note, and twice he made it moan
like a heart that's torn.
If done right, what tells the story, short or long,
is also in the music and its beat,
and I'd had enough of his hard-strummed song.
They finally roused my ire, those lower-pounding notes,
and the way he stressed his words:

Swift was the thrust with a spear, at once
                    bursting the neck of the warrior,
uttering a groan as he fell to the ground;
                    and the blood that he...

I asked him to stop
as I started down the stairs, two maidservants alongside.
Unpleased, he did as he was told,
leaving the story he was weaving
                              hanging in mid-air.

WAKEFUL DREAMING

These days I follow a path
straightway into wakeful dreaming.
The wind rises, and I sink,
and imagine a black, smooth-sailing ship
approaching Ithaca.
The wind subsides, and I dream on,
hearing a man's footsteps moving closer:
through these halls again he shall walk,
faithful Argos barking in the background.

Another year has come full round,
and in my mind's great meanderings
trying to understand why my husband in due season
has not returned,
I've nowhere to go but to believe
it's Odysseus striding through the palace,
husband I love all the way to the moon.
His leaving is the tears behind my eyes.

Back-to-back nights play upon the mind,
nights fading into the mounting rose-blush
of yet another dawn.
Soon upon me comes the light
marked by the mid-day blazing of the sun,
easing into afternoon, where the colors of twilight
loom in my sight. Then dark again...darkness.
What's the use—my days get spent that way.
No wind can blow back the years gone by.

With hope spread to its limits, may this day
come to an end.
Go ahead, deadly archer, Artemis divine,

make them whistle through the air
and their aim be true—
a quiver of arrows launched from your silver bow
finding their mark,
here,
the center of my heart.

SPEAKING AS MOTHER

Eyes closed,
I bore down and pushed, breath coming short
...but pushed some more.
And then, from my belly, emerged a morning sun

—that's how Telemachus crowned, and rose from me,
beautiful, in painless birth. Divine Eileithyia,
divine Artemis, a hundred-fold I blessed them;
and in my arms, my son.
My one thought—: he'll rise to fill a doorway like his father,
shoulders just as broad.
And so I nursed him sweetly, setting it my task
to make him know the well-shared customs of Achaeans.
I'm sorry for the mother who, by herself, has had to raise a son,
her husband off at war
—I've done my best.

"Careful not to smother him with love." The voice
was Eurycleia's, clear from across the room.
She went on, unwinding balls of purple, black, and yellow yarn,
placing them in different baskets for my tasks.
"Let him go from your watchful gaze, dear queen;
see to it he makes decisions on his own."
I understood her caring ways, and agreed to let him play
and roam around the palace grounds, the nearby fields,
playful Argos bounding at his heels.

Boys being what they are:
at eight he turned some sticks and stones
into a little bow and arrow for his games;
climbed a pear tree—twelve he must've been—
and reaching out for big bright fruit on the farthest bough,
fell and scraped his arm, tears hitting the ground.

Not much later, a burgeoning boy by then,
went off to help Laertes with a retaining wall
at his well-tilled farm.

"All that lifting, stone upon stone set in place
nine days straight, has made my arms and shoulders
strong," he said on his return.
"My working hands...look how calloused they've become.
Mother, when father finally does come home,
I could easily be his helper every day...just you wait."

Telemachus...darling son Telemachus
—the love I've poured into that boy, blood of my blood,
bone of my bones.
All the more unnerving his taking off to Sparta and to Pylos,
emboldened by his twenty years,
gone to ask his father's whereabouts.
I should've seen it coming days ago when,
sitting in his father's seat, he addressed a citizens assembly,
took a stand against the suitors set against me
like hounds after a fawn,
then ordered me away from his affairs.

Telemachus...Telemachus. He too is gone.
Twice-burdened and alone, I, Penelope,
sit waiting for two men—men I love madly.

NIGHTMARE

What once had been a soothing dream
has turned around—
no longer am I strolling at my ease by the water's edge,
sandals off,
the pleasure of sand to bare feet,
desiring everything to break my way.

Instead I'm on a ship,
sitting to the oar, and heading out to sea.
I row and row...can't steer straight.
Now the ship moves forward, now I'm veering east,
then wandering west and not alone: women, a crew of them
alongside and behind me, rowing, rowing.
The sea, now rough, begins to undulate in swells,
and when I again glance back—the nightmare of nightmares:
suitors, not the women, are poised at the oars;
but neither they nor I are rowing...the ship drifting
through mist.
By now I'm bathed in spray, and yelling out.
I yell again: "My son Telemachus,
without telling me, departed on his own.
Without telling us, has fled to sandy Pylos and to Sparta."

That's when I wake up in a cold sweat, startled
by what I've said into the night.

WHAT THE SPIRIT SAID

Clouds upon clouds piled up one day.
Then came an island of sunlight
                    pouring down to bring me hope.
That very day it rose upon my mind
to gather all my wits against the suitors swarming in.
Eurycleia and maidservants counted off the figures
collected in the great hall: one hundred total
added to a rank of eight more desiring faces
who gave no signs of drawing back.

Even now,
I can no more stop these men from paying court to me
than I can step away from my own shadow,
bringing much distress at the level of the heart,
although I try to never let it show.
Such turbulence
                    they've come around and caused.
But we live our lives by the habits we acquire,
so never may I be hostile to a guest. Xenia, we call it,
in the tongue of the Achaeans.

Desperation had closed in—
no way to put them off: their hands holding gifts;
their arms reaching out with wild intent.
Right then a spirit flowed into my head
to weave-and-weave to my heart's content a shroud
for Laertes, which I undid at night.
Weaving, unweaving and waiting I wove—
avoidance of the suitors was my mischief all those years.

One day I asked myself if
mine was a senseless heart;
if, for an instant, I'd lost the soundness of my mind.

Then, too, I wondered: had it been folly
to push this trick of the shroud too far?
What will people mutter
throughout time when they bring my name around?
After I'm gone,
what will ring in the ears of the unborn?
Here and now I say: I've done no ill.
No ill to crass and boorish men who know
nothing about weaving anyway, nor the time it takes to
run-the-shuttle-through-and-tie-the-final-knot on woven wool.

Three years...three years fully I rejoiced,
until my tattle-tale, malevolent maidservants turned me in—
those tarts.

ATHENA, SPINNER OF MANY SCHEMES

Must I wait for the gods' own time
to get Odysseus back,
man of commanding, calm demeanor?
If you know his whereabouts,
why not confide to me the place?
Give me, why not, as birds, the gift of flight
that I may search after him in forests, mountain ranges,
caves.
Come through, Athena, tell me in words plain:
can a man twenty years absent be yet alive,
and likely to return, pick up again
where he left off?

Pallas Athena,
grant my story gladness and bright glow—
race forth to me my husband
on a sailing-ship, I say,
make want and weariness forever
                              fade away.

LOVE BOUND

The sun rose,
blossomed into brightness, then took its time
heading toward the center of the sky. There it stood,
solitary, keeping its place,
glaring down until
the shadowed spaces were on the move again;
by which time I was bored, hungry,
so I had a bite to eat.
While the maids on their knees
kept grinding and sifting wheat and barley grain,
heaping handsful cupped together
(six-hundred someone said)
measured into baskets big,
and grumbling they were, all the while,
working masses of dough into flat loaves for the fire,
I slept,
and awoke at the moment when the sea was glazed
with red-becoming-orange—it was Helios
at the end of his run on the horizon's precipice,
then was gone.

In my room and around the palace, darkness abounds,
my mind sitting in shadow when two thoughts
come to light: that out of love bound together
by whatever binds together love over time,
I can wait for Odysseus, the man I like to think is mine alone;
that whatever lives in me, I call love—
true-wife love kept deep in the bone,
where only a wife can know it.

TWENTY YEARS WAITING

Just when I thought the star-lights of love
no longer shone for me, that I'd stand apart,

a woman, living more on lament than on hope,
down the stairs into the hall I went to see

the beggar-man, who the day before had walked
straight into my gaze; who was no stranger begging,

but truly Odysseus, the man I love the way a woman
does just the one time. From the moment we stepped

into our room, into a claiming embrace, teary-eyed,
joyful in a reaching 'round of arms, I knew it

in my heart as a wife would know she's finally
home with her husband, the agony of love no more.

Lovers long estranged, we drank and drank, stopped
...and yet again drank from our kisses. I thanked

thrice the gods, thanked the sea. Then came desire
washing over me, and I melted at the knees, tunics

falling from us at the foot of our olive-tree bed—
body awakened as when, by the fluttering of wings,

a caged bird still recalls flight. I'd been for years at
the heart's low-ebb, but wise about men set before me,

and gods disguised. Now the man long-awaited
had washed ashore into my room: I opened my eyes

and saw, past the ceiling, an expanse of sky
and Odysseus sailing steadily above me. In the life

of two bodies, one sets in motion the other, both
moving to the meaning of husband and wife

after twenty years waiting. And what we uttered took
love that much higher; made it ascend to heights

of delight where no sound could be heard, save
the sound of two lovers in a room full of love

where husband and wife finally arrived, moored to
each other, at the dreamed-of, the imagined, the absolute

moment of rapture, beyond words, sweet to our mortal
taste. O astonished and exalted heart when, before it,

is revealed that hoping against hope has yielded
its reward. To him, last night, all of me I gave. Athena

had reined in the horses of dawn, and drawn out the night.
Daybreak—and the first touches of color still found us

wrapped in each other's arms, Odysseus and I, wordless,
in the wisdom that love, as ever, is the light we live by.

Photo: © 2009 Mike Howard

TINO VILLANUEVA is the author of six books of poetry, among them *Shaking Off the Dark* (1984); *Crónica de mis años peores* (1987) / *Chronicle of My Worst Years* (1994); *Scene from the Movie GIANT* (1993), which won a 1994 American Book Award; and *Primera causa / First Cause* (1999), a chapbook on memory and writing. Villanueva has been anthologized in *An Ear to the Ground: An Anthology of Contemporary American Poetry* (1989), *Poetas sin fronteras* (2000), and most recently in *The Norton Anthology of Latino Literature* (2011). He has taught creative writing at the University of Texas–Austin, The College of William & Mary, and Bowdoin College. His art work has appeared on the covers and pages of national and international journals, such as *Nexos, Green Mountains Review, TriQuarterly, Parnassus,* and *MELUS.* He teaches in the Department of Romance Studies at Boston University.

So Spoke Penelope was set in Garamond, a group of old style serif typefaces named for the punch-cutter Claude Garamond (c. 1480–1561). Garamond came to prominence in 1540 in France. Revivals of the Garamond type can be found as early as 1900, when a typeface was introduced at the Paris World's Fair as "Original Garamond."

In 1984, Garamond was adopted by Apple Computer upon the release of Macintosh. The fonts are known as Apple Garamond.

So Spoke Penelope was printed in an edition of 800 copies by Thomson-Shore Inc., Dexter, Michigan, in January 2013, and reprinted in an edition of 800 in January 2014.

The cover art is by Richard McLaughlin, work untitled.